MOVED TO A NEW MINDSET

21 DAYS DEVOTIONAL

Donna M. Morris

MOVED TO A NEW MINDSET

21 DAYS DEVOTIONAL

DAILY ENCOURAGEMENT FOR THE TRANSFORMED MIND

RESTORATION OF THE BREACH
WITHOUT BORDERS

West Palm Beach, Florida

DONNA M. MORRIS

Moved to a New Mindset 21 Days Devotional

Copyright © 2021 Donna M. Morris

ISBN: 978-1-954755-55-0

Published by:
Restoration of the Breach without Borders
133 45th Street, Building A7
West Palm Beach, Florida 33407
restorativeauthor@gmail.com
Tele: (561) 388-2949

EBook Cover Design by:
Leostone Morrison
restorativeauthor@gmail.com

Editing done by:
Melisha Bartley-Ankle
melbarxtd@yahoo.com

Formatting and Publishing done by:
Sherene Morrison
Publisher.20@aol.com

Dedication

This devotional is dedicated to my four biological sisters, Patricia, Pauline, Winsome and Murna.

Thank you for always believing in me.

You have been a source of inspiration and strength on my journey.

I am so blessed to have your love and support. The encouragement you bring is priceless. I sincerely love each of you.

You are indeed a true epitome of strong women, every day you rise with vision and purpose.. You are queens.

There is so much that God has in store for you all.

My greatest desire is that you will read this book and experience the super abundance that the Lord has packaged for you. Choose to win in your mind and let your new mindset become a reality.

Your new way of thinking will give you a new way of living.

Donna Morris
"Moved to a New Mindset: Free From Limitations, Rejections, And Fears"

Acknowledgements

"This is the Lord's doing and it is marvellous in our eyes'. Psalms 118:23

I am grateful to the Holy Spirit for his faithful guidance and giving me the grace to walk by faith on this journey of Moving to a new mindset.

Thank you, Lord, for your undeserving blessings and continuous favour in my life. Thank you for writing this book, I am your yielded vessel, and I am thankful for the lives that this devotional will be impacting.

To my loving husband Donald Morris, and my son Damari Morris who continues to be a source of strength and support as the assignments from the Lord increases. I extend heartfelt gratitude.

To my blessed and beautiful family. Thank you for the overwhelming support you have shown to me.It has not been an easy journey, but God has kept me going.

Special appreciation to Bishop Sharon Prince for your endorsement. Your prayerful support along with "A Time of Together Ministries" is beyond calculation.

Thank you, Bridget Elesin you have come into my life, for such a time as this. Your kind words of endorsement are really appreciated.

Melisha Bartley-Ankle, thank you for allowing the Lord to use you. Your creative input on editing of the manuscript is appreciated.

To Eric Hosin, your support along with my Guardian Life Family has never ceased since the publication of my first book. Sir, I thank you for writing the foreword.

Words cannot express my appreciation to Rev Leostone Morrison and Sherene Morrison.

Thank you for working tirelessly, being a constant source of encouragement in making the publication of this book a reality. You are indeed destiny helpers. May God richly bless your selfless efforts.

I sincerely thank my Church Family at Church of the United Missions. And my pastor, the Reverend Conrad Thomas for their support and encouragement. Much shout out to the   Marriage Ministry Fellowship. Thanks for your prayerful support and encouragement in all I do.

I give God all the glory and praise to help me persevere in spite of the odds.

Without the constant presence of the Holy Spirit reviving, me and igniting me to keep going. I would not fill the pages with the messages within this book,

Lord, I love you and I bless you with my whole heart.

Foreword

I am humbled and delighted to write this foreword.

Donna Morris, fellow Life Guardian, and Kingdom Ambassador. This is indeed a great accomplishment despite the challenging seasons we are experiencing.

Congratulations Donna, for the journey of Moving to a New Mindset.

The Mind is a very powerful asset, for it is the foundation of everything and it determines the way we live. This 21-day devotional will motivate and encourage you as it gives daily messages that will assist you with the renewing of the mind.

"And be renewed in the spirit of your mind" Ephesians 4:23.

This book also challenges readers to view obstacles as learning experiences and that they can embrace a new way of thinking...

Donna expresses that the challenges of the mind are real, and you can start your day by meditating on God's words.

Moved to a New Mindset 21-day devotional is no ordinary book my friends.

It is a book for all seasons, you will not be disappointed. You will be blessed and inspired on your 21-day journey and beyond.

--Eric Hosin
Guardian Life Limited
Group head,
Life, Health & Pensions

Endorsements

Dear reader,

Your mind is likened to your seat of power for as you think in your heart, so you become. If you think on thoughts that are lovely and of good report, you live a better life than when you think thoughts of lack, fear and challenges that keep you from making progress.

In the 21 days moved to a new mindset devotional by Minister Donna Morris, you will learn how to read God's words, plus pray as you move from an unproductive way of thinking to a productive and progressive new way of thinking.

The 21 days covers various aspect of life as she trains readers on how to declutter their minds of negative thought patterns and think godly thoughts that will help them in their day-to-day life.

I love how simple and easy to read the devotional is, I love the stories she tells to buttress why we need to have the right mindset and I love the prayers at the end of each day's devotional.

This is a devotional that will elevate you to thinking, living and doing better in every way as you start or end your day reading God's words.

-Bridget Elesin
Marriage and family life
practitioner.
Author - Fathers, you must take
the lead

******

Your mind is like a garden, you kill snakes, you pull weeds, and you plant beautiful flowers. Your mind is your world and it's your greatest investment. Donna Morris in her *"Moved to A New Mindset" 21 Days Devotional* is a MUST read. One chapter a day is like taking your medication.

It will definitely Kickstart your day and set you on a path of no return.

Moved to a New Mindset 21 Days Devotional

I endorse this devotion for daily living.Shalom, unstoppable author Donna Morris

-Bishop Sharon Prince
A TIME OF Togetherness
Ministries International

Table of Contents

Dedication iv

Acknowledgements vi

Foreword ix

Endorsements xi

Introduction 1

Appetizer 3

Day 1: A Cup of Prayer 4

Day 2: Declutter 6

Day 3: Train Your Mind 9

Day 4: Control Your Thoughts 12

Day 5: Victory Over Negative Thoughts 14

Day 6: No Limits, No Boundaries 17

Day 7: Guard Your Words 20

Day 8: Bent but Not Broken 23

Day 9: You Are Valuable 26

Day 10: Keep Pressing 29

Day 11: Refuel 32

Day 12: Remove the Mask 34

Day 13: Watch Your Weight 37

Day 14: Who Do I Need to Forgive?   40

Day 15: Give Your Burdens to God   43

Day 16: Preserved in The Fire   45

Day 17: Storms? Do Not Panic   48

Day 18: Do Not Disqualify Yourself   51

Day 19: Make Bold Moves   54

Day 20: God Will Answer   57

Day 21: Crossover Now   59

21 Days of   62

Transforming Affirmations   62

About the Author   68

You do not have to remain where you are. Whether it is discouragement, negative self-talk, or a quest to grow deeper in faith, kick-start your day by seeking God through these 21 days of inspiration. *Moved to a New Mindset Devotional* is designed to offer encouragement, strength and most importantly, victory for the transformed mind.

Introduction

Since the publication of my first book, *Moved to a New Mindset Free from Limitations, Rejections and Fears,* I have received an overwhelming number of praise reports from people all over the world, who the book has impacted. It still amazes me that so many take the time to pen their thoughts and share with me how they have been liberated from the truths shared in my book. I am deeply grateful and humbled to have been able to be part of their lives in such an intimate way and for having the opportunity to share that it is the Lord's doing that has brought transformation and freedom in my mind!

Moved to a New Mindset Devotional has been purposefully designed to allow you to spend just five to ten minutes per day reading God's Word.

Take note that this devotional is written to edify and encourage you on a path of moving forward in victory. When you begin your new mindset journey, it

1

will always keep you moving forward. The reality is that most people will live a life of defeat because instead of looking to God they focus on the daily challenges and become discouraged. However, living victoriously requires faith and an ability to follow God's directive.

My friend, time spent with God is never wasted! In spite of your hectic schedule or the challenges you face, devote a few minutes each day to commune with the Lord. Let the 21-day devotional guide you on this journey. While it can be personal, the devotional is also geared towards small groups, family, or church setting. This book will draw you confidently toward God's plans and purposes for you as His beloved. So, fasten your seat belt, change your thoughts, change your life, face the battles, and lay hold on victory.

Appetizer

Let the journey begin…

BATTLE OF THE MIND

No one is immune to the battle of the mind; it is a universal enemy that we all must fight. However, take heart, freedom and by extension victory is possible. In the world's armies, soldiers must be fully trained before entering the battlefield; they endure months of serious training in order to be physically and mentally fit. They are also trained to handle different wartime tactics of the enemy. Likewise, Ephesians 6 reminds us that we daily fight against the wiles of the devil but with the full armour and God as our captain we are fully equipped for the challenge. Let us get into God's Word today.

Day 1
A Cup of Prayer

'O God, thou art my God; early will I seek
thee: my soul thirsteth for thee, my flesh
longeth for thee in a dry and thirsty land,
where no water is' (Psalms 63:1)

*E*very morning, the alarm goes off and you wake up.

However, do not take it for granted, the true source of
your waking is not the alarm but the faithful grace of
God. With that reality, how do you really prepare
your mind to greet each day? Are you delighted to
meet with God in prayer? If you spend time with
Him, do you value each moment or do you routinely
rattle off a few words as you rush through the door?

If you are wise you will form a habit of spending
quality time with God. Begin your day with the
Father, read His word, pray and give Him worship.
Once you get into the presence of the Lord in the

early morning it will align your priorities and prepare your mindset by giving you the needed strength and courage for the day. You may have a great deal to do but carve out time for God; think about His goodness and grace.

Prioritise God. Seek Him early and pant after His presence. Let Him be at the forefront of your mind. Do not be distracted with checking your phone, emails or social media. While many things are craving your attention, you can have a winning start by beginning your day with God.

BITE OF THE DAY

Let God be the first person you talk to each day.

REFLECTION

Have you renewed your mind by talking to God?

Day 2
Declutter

'Behold, I will do a new thing; now it shall spring forth; shall ye not know it? I will even make a way in the wilderness, and rivers in the desert' (Isaiah 43:19).

*D*uring my childhood years, my mother always told me to clean my room and get rid of the old things. As human beings we love to hoard. Therefore, it is important to always take time to clean out the old stuff from our houses, cars, and any place that junk may clutter. At times it may seem as though everything is sentimentally attached. I have clothes that I have not worn for years and although they were taking up space in the closet, I just could not get rid of them; I was not ready to declutter. Nevertheless, I had to make an intentional move in my mind; they were precious, but it was time to part with them. I had to make the choice to let go of the old things.

Likewise, a very difficult assignment to undertake is to purge the mind from past events. Imagine if we were to continually replay every hurt, abuse, or disappointment then we will definitely be mentally immobilized. The hurt, the pain is simply taking up space in our minds so that we become imprisoned by the spirit of bitterness and unforgiveness. The truth is it takes courage to lay aside the weight that we have carried around for years and in many instances, we cannot do it alone. We need God to help us release the load of the past. We cannot experience newness while carrying junk. Now is the time to clean out the old things in our minds. Clear out all wrong thinking, past hurts, doubts and embrace the truth of God's word.

God has good things in store that He wants to give us. However, to experience such victory! Say goodbye to the Old and welcome the New!

BITE OF THE DAY

Newness begins by getting rid of the junk and making room for the things God has for us.

REFLECTION

How often do you clear the junk from your mind?

Day 3
Train Your Mind

'Study to shew thyself approved unto God, a
workmanship that needeth not to be ashamed
rightly dividing the Word of truth' 2
Timothy 2:15.

So, then faith cometh by hearing, and
hearing by the word of God. Romans 10:17

*S*oldiers going into battle must undergo rigorous

training in order to be prepared. Like the soldiers in
the physical army, we too have a battle. Therefore, it
is imperative to understand that if you do not engage
your mind in training, you cannot be ready for
spiritual warfare; It is just impossible to make
progress. It is important that you fervently train your
mind by studying the Word of truth. How can you
walk by faith unless you know God's word?

The scripture expresses that faith comes by hearing the word. Be serious about studying your Bible. Set your mind on the Word of God and be intentional in biblical affirmations. Begin to repeat the Word over yourself. 'I am blessed and highly favoured, I am an Overcomer, I am walking by faith and not by sight.'

God has instructed us to spend time in his word every day so our faith can grow. Listen to his voice while you read for, He has much to say to you. The Holy Spirit will always communicate to you through the pages of scripture. When the word of God begins to come alive God is speaking to you. Therefore, listen carefully so that the Lord can communicate to you. Embrace the discipline of memorizing

passages of scripture and watch your life transform. How can you practice the word of God unless you remember it? Bind it in your heart! Then, as you begin to practice the word God will meet with you. Stay attentive to God's voice that He may show you exactly how and when to apply His word.

BITE OF THE DAY

Train your mind to face all challenges with faith.

REFLECTION

How important is it to train your mind?

Day 4
Control Your Thoughts

Set your mind on things above, not on
earthly things. Colossians 3:2

*A*re you struggling with distraction? You are not

alone, it is something that mankind has been dealing
with since the beginning of time. One minute you are
bent on completing a task the next your mind just
keeps wandering; I have been there. I can recall times
of prayer where I was really connecting with God
then I began thinking about what I was going to cook
for dinner; it happens to the best of us.

Therefore, Paul instructs us to set our minds on things
above and not on earthly things, in essence control
your thoughts. Our thought life guides our actions
therefore it is super important that we surrender our
entire thought process to God. Do not allow
distractions to set in and take you away from the task

at hand. The enemy knows that prayer is powerful but if he is able to distract you from spending quality time with God then he would have robbed you of that power.

With that knowledge let us set our thoughts on what is true, honorable, right, pure, lovely and admirable. Think about things that are excellent and worthy of praise. Philippians 4:8. Begin to make the right choice. Give yourself to the Holy Spirit, let Him help you. Be Intentional. Spend time in prayer. Read God's Word. Surrender your thoughts to Him and practice speaking positive affirmations

BITE OF THE DAY

Your thoughts are the steering wheel of your life, choose to take control of them!

REFLECTION

Who or what controls your mind?

Day 5
Victory Over Negative Thoughts

"Casting down imaginations, and every high
thing that exalteth itself against the
knowledge of God and bringing into
captivity every thought to the obedience of
Christ;" 2 Corinthians 10:5.

Our thoughts have the power to control us. Whatever
we entertain in our minds is certainly what we will
reap-*Moved to a New Mindset.*

*F*or us to have victory over negative thoughts we

must be intentional in thinking about things that are
aligned to the scriptures:

"Finally, brethren, whatsoever things are
true, whatsoever things are honest,
whatsoever things are just, whatsoever
things are pure, whatsoever things are

lovely, whatsoever things are of good report; if there be any virtue, and if there be any praise, think on these things" Philippians 4:8.

Oftentimes the enemy will shoot negative thoughts about who I am into my mind. Thereafter feelings of insecurity will come knocking. If I receive the thoughts, then I begin to think that life as a whole is negative. Therefore, I must be decisive. I must choose to close my mind's door to the enemy and his plans. You can have victory over negative thoughts starting today.

- Identify the negative thoughts in your mind,
- Dismiss the negative thoughts from your mind
- Replace the negative thoughts with the word of God.

Change the way you think it will change the way you feel and soon after your whole life will change.

Thought: You do not have to remain defeated in your mind. Choose to defeat negative thoughts.

BITE OF THE DAY

What do you usually do with them?

REFLECTION

Are you able to recognize negative thoughts when they come?

Day 6
No Limits, No Boundaries

"For God has not given us a spirit of fear, but of power, love and a sound mind." II Timothy 1:7

*A*fter publishing *'Moved to a New Mindset, Free from Limitations, Rejections and Fears"* I still struggled with maintaining a mind free from limitations. The battle of the mind is never ending so the old thoughts would occasionally come begging me to let them in. I remember being at work in a department meeting when the question was asked if anyone had anything to say. I had something to say but I literally wrestled with thoughts of fears and doubts, not wanting to speak.

For too long I have had a relationship with impoverished thoughts that caused me to wade in so much doubt. I was trapped into thinking that I could

17

not achieve much and that it was all there was to life. Thankfully things have changed. I now have the power to identify the limited thoughts that are lurking and refuse to let them in. I have conquered my fears by stepping out and speaking up. When you take the limits off your mind you choose to change the way you think. Renew your mind. Refocus your thoughts and embrace God's purpose.

You must make the choice to take the limits off your mind. Fears no longer have to bully you to keep quiet. The Word of God has power to activate and transform your mind. Do not be passive, sitting back allowing doubts and fears to influence your life. Choose to dwell on what the scripture says in Philippians 4:8.

Get up each day and think of the wonderful things that God has in store for you. Boldly declare" Father I am excited about today," This is the day you have made; I am going to rejoice and be glad in it" Psalms 118:24. Take the limits off your mind.

BITE OF THE DAY

Your mind is your private property, do not allow thoughts of doubts to trespass.

REFLECTION

Are you able to identify limited thoughts when they approach your mind?

Day 7
Guard Your Words

Proverbs 18:21 says, "Death and life are in the power of the tongue, and they that love it shall eat the fruit thereof."

Your thoughts and words set the tone for your day.

Therefore, even before you get out of bed choose to put a watch on what you think and speak. Scripture tells us that our words are both powerful and creative. As a result, it is imperative that we learn to use the life-giving wisdom given in God's word to purposefully build our lives and that of others. When you do, your life and that of others in your surrounding will never be the same.

Always pay attention to your words. Matthew 12:37 declares, 'For by thy words thou shalt be justified, and by thy words thou shalt be condemned.' Our words not only reflect our thoughts, but they also shape our world. In the same manner this universe is held together by God's words, our words, whether negative or positive, determine the life we live. Begin to guard your words by constantly infusing the Word of God in your mind and by doing so negativity will not be able to take root in your life.

If you are struggling with being negative, critical, or judgmental of people and situations do not be discouraged; there is hope for you today. God wants to change your life by transforming your words. It may not happen overnight but each day you will make progress as you choose to allow the Holy Spirit to put a guard on your words. It is time for you to experience and enjoy the life God created you to live by speaking life.

BITE OF THE DAY

Do not speak defeat over yourself. The words you prophesy either give life or death to your circumstances; they are what you become

REFLECTION

Who can you encourage today? Be intentional in speaking life to others.

Day 8
Bent but Not Broken

The righteous shall flourish like the palm
tree; he shall grow like a cedar in Lebanon

Psalms 92:12

I remember watching the palm tree during a

hurricane. When the winds came it bent but quickly
bounced back because its root is strong and resilient
in weathering the storm. Interestingly, after the
hurricane, the palm tree is stronger than before.
Scripture shows us that we are in an ongoing spiritual
warfare, and we must be prepared for imaginations
and strongholds in the mind 2 Corinthians 10:4-5.
Mental walls will try to stop you, but it does not
matter the size wall that may come to hinder you from
advancing in the things of God, you can demolish
them. Stay in faith! You do not have to break.

Winds of negative criticism may come your way, but you can still jump over every hurdle and flourish. Certainly, the storms of life may be numerous, but you do not have to stay down. Now is not the time to be defeated. Be resilient on this journey of Moving to a New Mindset! Remember who you are and know that your faith in God will allow you to bend but do not break. You are righteous and you will always flourish like the palm tree. You may even be criticized for leaving your comfort zone. Disappointments and setbacks may come but the key is to maintain a transformed mind. From time to time, you may bend but be a palm tree that speaks. Tell the winds that you will not break. Look out! The winds are coming against you to rob your joy, peace, and victory but once you are rooted like the palm tree you will stand, flourish, and grow strong in the Lord.

BITE OF THE DAY

You are a strong Palm tree. Remain rooted in challenging winds.

REFLECTION

Do you easily bend and break when the winds of criticism blow?

Day 9
You Are Valuable

'I will praise thee; for I am fearfully and wonderfully made marvellous are thy works; and that my soul knoweth right well' Psalms 139:14.

*A*s my husband and I entered the jewelry store to look at the wedding rings, we observed that some were of a greater value. As a result, it was not easy deciding on which ring to choose. Finally, we decided on one that really caught our eyes, but the truth is all the rings in the showcase were valuable.

You are valuable in God's eyes. You are a masterpiece in His hand. You may not even fully understand YOUR VALUE RIGHT NOW but do not be perturbed. You may have experienced a few cracks and bruises but that will not lower your value. You are still here. You are blessed by God to live! Yes,

26

you are. God specializes in transforming imperfect vessels into valuable ones. Guess what? God is ready and committed to work on you. Allow Him to use His words to correct and comfort you! The Master Potter is more than capable of making a complete work of art out of you. Phil 1:6 Being confident of this very thing that He who began a good work is able to complete it.

As you move to a new mindset, hold this truth, there is great value in you. It does not matter how marred, bruised or imperfect you may be right now. God is the architect of your life, and He finds great worth in you. Always remember you are valuable. Your uniqueness is embedded in your flaws. Yes, God wants to use you just as you are. He looks at you through the lens of his love. A part of 1 Corinthians Chapter 13 states charity suffereth long and is patient.

Look at God's heart for you. He wants you to see that He places great value on you. You are blessed. You are favoured. You are wonderfully made. Do not forget you are valuable.

BITE OF THE DAY

You are extremely valuable in God's sight.

REFLECTION

Do you compare yourself to others?

Day 10
Keep Pressing

'And a certain woman, which had an issue of blood twelve years. And had suffered many things of many physicians, and had spent all that she had, and was nothing bettered, but rather grew worse, when she had heard of Jesus, came in the press behind, and touched his garment' Mark 5:25-27.

*T*he woman with the issue of blood had struggled

with her infirmity for many years. She had been to many physicians, but she got progressively worse. Then she heard that Jesus was passing her way and was determined to get close to touch Him. Irrespective of the obstacles, she was adamant that she had to press through the crowd and receive her deliverance. The mental battle must have been tremendous, but the woman stepped out in faith, pressed past her limitations, and received her healing.

God has a deliverance just for you. However, you need to press into His presence. You need to transform your mind. Draw closer to God so that you can touch Him. Do you notice that every achievement comes with obstacles? However, do not stop. Keep going. Faith is what you wear every day so you can touch God.

"But without faith it is impossible to please him: for he that cometh to God must believe that he is, and that he is a rewarder of them that diligently seek him" Hebrews 11:6.

BITE OF THE DAY

Be determined to keep pressing. Remember your feet cannot go where your mind as not been

REFLECTION

Are you looking at your situation from a position of fear or faith?

Day 11
Refuel

'But they that wait upon the Lord shall
renew their strength; they shall mount up
with wings as eagles; they shall run, and not
be weary; and they shall walk, and not faint'
Isaiah 40:31.

'I must check the engine, and have it refueled,'

those were my husband's words as he prepared for his
long journey to the country a few years ago. The truth
is vehicles always need to be refueled. If you drive
and never stop to refill the gas tank you may soon be
stranded on the highway with a problem, you could
have avoided.

Consider yourself on life's journey. You will need to
have your strength renewed in order to function
effectively. Many of us do not take time to pour into
ourselves. We believe it is wrong to have quiet time!

Time to relax. Take a break. Have fun… Spend time with the family; that is a great way to refuel. Have some good laughs and enjoy yourself. Do not take life too seriously! Taking care of your mental space is a very important way to refuel.

God has blessed us, and He wants us to enjoy His blessings! Take a vacation and celebrate the goodness of God. Do not let others intimidate you that you are afraid to take a break from the busyness of life. Dress up! Show up at an event and just have fun. Do not neglect your life. **Refuel!**

BITE OF THE DAY

A transformed mind understands what it means to take time off.

REFLECTION

How have you been treating yourself? When was the last time you refueled?

Day 12
Remove the Mask

Casting all your cares upon him, for he
careth for you. 1 Peter 5:7

*D*uring the pandemic it was mandatory that we wore

masks to protect ourselves from the Coronavirus.
Now the restrictions from the pandemic have
gradually been lifted. However, many people are still
wearing a mask. A different kind of mask. The mask
of hurt and rejection that many are not even aware of.

While there are many hurting people in our
community, family, church, and society we are
unaware of their pain because they wear a mask. They
may be longing for deliverance but unless they
remove the mask, they cannot be free. Freedom is
yours but you must be honest about the past hurts, the
hidden scars of rejections and the effect it may have
on your life. Genuine confession to God and letting

go of unforgiveness can be the start to take the mask off.

For too long many of us have tried to deal with our pain by hiding behind good appearance, false impressions, or spirituality. Masks come in various sizes and shapes, but they must be removed. God wants to do a work of transformation in your life but are you ready to remove the mask? Only you can make that choice. I have removed the mask of limitations in the mind and have experienced a mind-blowing renewal. I am not ashamed to talk about it. I was one of those persons who appeared ok. However, I was struggling with impoverished thoughts for years. Thank God I got my breakthrough and God wants to do the same for you today. It is really time to remove your mask. Yes! The Lord can transform any circumstance. Just remove your mask.

BITE OF THE DAY

God can do the impossible in your life.

REFLECTION

Have you been hiding behind a mask in order to conceal pain, secret scars or fear?

Day 13
Watch Your Weight

'Wherefore seeing we also are compassed about with so great a cloud of witnesses, let us lay aside every weight, and the sin which doth so easily beset us, and let us run with patience the race that is set before us'
Hebrews 12:1.

Remember the mind is the faculty of man's reasoning and thoughts – Chris Oyakhilome

*M*onitoring our weight is very important. Excess weight can cause severe complications in our health. Therefore, it is important that we watch what we eat and be intentional about maintaining a proper diet and regular exercise. It is crucial that we stay away from foods that are high in fat, sugar and have large amounts of preservatives with little or no nutritional value. Likewise, each day we must continually monitor what we allow to enter our spirit and how we respond to people and situations.

A harsh word spoken to our spouse, a frown to our coworker or being impatient with our child or children can cause unnecessary heaviness. When you begin to pay attention to your spiritual weight you will know when you are offended by others. Unfortunately, if you do not learn to let go, unforgiveness will fester and said spirit will only cause weight gain. It is time to lay aside every baggage in your life. Whether it is bitterness, wrath, clamour, evil speaking or malice, Ephesians 4:30, you must make a concerted effort to put negativity out of your life. In other words, it is time to lose the weight.

Your transformed mind will bloom as you begin to spend quality time, whether in private or collective worship, ingesting the Word of God.

BITE OF THE DAY

The state of your mindset will determine what you allow in your life.

REFLECTION

Do you pay attention to your weight?

Day 14
Who Do I Need to Forgive?

'But if ye do not forgive, neither will your
Father which is in heaven may forgive you
your trespasses' Mark 11:25.

*A*s you begin each day prepare your mind to forgive.

On life's journey we must be constantly forgiving
others. It is a deliberate practice that has to be learnt
and implemented on a regular basis.

My life has drastically changed since I began
practicing extending grace when others have offended
me. It is a real battle in the mind but with the power
of the Holy Spirit you can undo grudges and let go of
the weight of unforgiveness.

The truth is, if you do not forgive others, you will not
receive forgiveness from your Heavenly Father.
Offense will come but what will you do with that

emotion? If you are offended and walking in the spirit of unforgiveness you need to repent of such sin in order to receive your freedom. Forgiveness makes a great future possible. The best way to start your day is by communing with God and in those daily moments ask the Holy Spirit, 'Who do I need to Forgive?" Bear in mind that forgiveness is not an option, it is compulsory for winning the mental battle and receive complete freedom.

Forgiving those who have wronged you is key to personal freedom. Without forgiveness your life will be governed by endless cycles of bitterness, resentment, and retaliation.

BITE OF THE DAY

Freedom in the mind always rests on the platform of forgiveness. It is time to Forgive.

REFLECTION

Have you checked your heart lately? Who do you need to forgive?

Day 15
Give Your Burdens to God

'Cast your burden upon the Lord and he will
sustain thee, He shall never suffer the
righteous to be moved' Psalms 55:22.

*I*f there is ever a time you need to cast your burdens

on the Lord is now. In these challenging times people
are extremely overwhelmed with varied burdens.
However, we were never designed to be burden
bearers. We were created in the image and likeness of
God, but sin brought burden on us. Therefore, God
had to make a way for us to be relieved of our burden
by sending his son Jesus Christ into the world to die
and bring us redemption.

'For God so Loved the world that he gave
his only begotten son that whosoever

believeth in him should not perish but have
everlasting life' St John 3: 16.

Whatever burden you may be facing today you can
cast it on the Lord. Regardless of the weight of the
load, Jesus is the only one that can truly relieve you
of the burden you are facing. Is it a financial burden?
Just give it to the Lord. Is it a burden of failure? Give
it to God as well. Do not allow the enemy to trick you
into thinking that you can manage on your own. Our
Loving Father wants us to turn all burdens over to
Him and leave them. It is time to let go of the
burdens.

BITE OF THE DAY

It is time to give your burdens to God.

REFLECTION

Are you carrying a load for which Jesus already paid
the price?

Day 16
Preserved in The Fire

'Look!" he answered, "I see four men loose, walking in the midst of the fire; and they are not hurt, and the form of the fourth is like the Son of God." And the satraps, administrators, governors, and the king's counselors gathered together, and they saw these men on whose bodies the fire had no power; the hair of their head was not singed nor were their garments affected, and the smell of fire was not on them' Daniel 3:25, 27 NKJV.

*A*t ten (10) years old I was told to wash the dishes.

While in the kitchen I noticed that there was intense heat coming from the oven. I wondered how my mother managed to stay in the kitchen with such heat. It is just amazing how we can go through fiery situations and God keeps us. As the three Hebrew boys were preserved when they were thrown into life's fiery furnace be assured that the God in whom you have professed faith will meet and keep you in your fire. He is the fourth Man in the midst right there with you!! God will be with you in every stage of your life. He is able to preserve you. The enemy knows that God wants to take care of you in the fiery circumstance, so he causes the fire to be more intense but do not surrender. Even when the fire is intensified faith will make you walk around and encounter the preserving presence of God.

There are certain hard seasons you will go through in life and God may choose not to remove you from it. However, He will stand with you as you navigate the fire. The Lord is watching over your life and regardless of the magnitude of the fire you will not be burnt.

YOU WILL NEVER LOOK LIKE WHAT YOU HAVE BEEN THROUGH BECAUSE YOU ARE PRESERVED BY AN ALL-POWERFUL GOD!!

BITE OF THE DAY

Regardless of the intensity of the heat God can preserve you in the fire.

REFLECTION

Do you sometimes feel alone in the furnace of challenges?

Day 17
Storms? Do Not Panic

'When thou passest through the waters, I will be with thee; and through the rivers, they shall not overflow thee: when thou walkest through the fire, thou shalt not be burned; neither shall the flame kindle upon thee' Isaiah 43:2.

*H*ave you ever noticed that the weather forecast may predict a storm that may or may not come? The truth is life is different. The storms of life are inevitable and come in different types.

Storms of life can happen suddenly. However, whatever the nature of the storm you can ride it out with faith and confidence that God is able to take you through. Put your trust in God and allow His Word to take root and grow in your life. As you face a storm do not panic!! It is not designed to kill you. It is a test.

A process to check and strengthen your relationship with God. As a result, do not fear because the Lord is very much present with you.

The storm's objective is to uproot you but if you remain grounded in Christ you can flip the script and become stronger. God knows the determination that He has deposited in you so do not panic, just ride out your storm. Stop stressing. Relax. God is with you. If you are experiencing a money storm, ride it out by confessing His Word and believe that it is going to work. God will supply your need Philippian 4:19.

If you are experiencing an enemy storm, do not panic ride it out with Psalm 46:7 The Lord of Hosts is with you the God of Jacob is your refuge.

Now is not the time to cower in fear or run away. Focus!! Keep your eyes on what God is doing in your life. If only you will understand that Jesus can speak to the storm and calm, it. Do not be distracted by circumstances that come your way to cause you to fear. In fact, the weather may become boisterous at times but do not allow fear to cause your boat to capsize...

BITE OF THE DAY

It does not matter the category storm that you are facing, it is temporary. It has an expiration date.

REFLECTION

How do you handle storms when they come?

Day 18
Do Not Disqualify Yourself

For we walk by faith and not by sight. 2
Corinthians 5:7

In 2017 I received the promise word to make a

move in my mind concerning home improvement

loan. However, I did not act on the word. In fact,

because I did not step out in faith and enquired about

the availability of the loan, I literally disqualified

myself. I was not even aware that if I did not step out

in faith I would remain in a state of disqualification.

If you hold on to doubt and fear, they will certainly

disqualify you. Today is the time to walk in faith and

not by sight. The moment God's word entered my

mind, and I received it freedom was mine. When

God speaks, many persons have neglected to make

that move of faith and have remained locked up in

51

their minds. Choose to Move in faith and do not disqualify yourself.

Decide to walk by faith and make bold steps toward God's plans for your life.

Whatever it is that you are in need of, step out in faith today.

God has great things in store for you today.

Be adamant that yesterday was the last day you saw yourself as unqualified. Do your part in stepping out in faith. Make that phone call. Send that email or just ask someone. It is time to arise in your mind. The truth is, you will never tread the path that your mind has not gone. With God showing up for me, I now understand that once you receive His Word and act upon it you will discover that you are more than qualified.

BITE OF THE DAY

Do not disqualify yourself, take that mental action today!

REFLECTION

How will you know if you are qualified if you do not even make an inquiry? How will you know if you will be accepted in college if you do not apply?

Day 19
Make Bold Moves

'And the Lord spake unto Moses, saying, go
in, speak unto Pharaoh king of Egypt, that he
let the children of Israel go out of his land.
And Moses spake before the Lord, saying,
Behold, the children of Israel have not
hearkened unto me; how then shall Pharaoh
hear me, who am of uncircumcised lips?'
Exodus 6;10-12.

*A*s I reflect on Moses, one of the greatest leaders in

the Old Testament, I recognize that he was filled with
excuses and inadequacies concerning what God had
called him to do. God had a big plan to use him
mightily but Moses, like most of us, was quick to
make excuses. We can be loaded with so many
excuses that immobilize us. Thwart us from making
bold moves in our lives.

Moses named all his flaws; the many reasons he was not able to do what God had already equipped him to do. Do not let fear rob you of making moves, job opportunities, college educations, and even ministry moments await. Whenever fear grips our hearts our knees may knock, our voice quivers, and we curl into our shells. But why? Why do we freeze up? Why does our boldness go through the window when God given opportunities or challenges confront us? God promised never to leave us, and He will give us boldness in the moment that we need it. Now is the time to step out in faith so that we can maximize our full potential.

Moses had his Pharaoh and David his Goliath. You have your challenges. Remember you are equipped for the task. Are you having feelings of fear? Begin to ask God for supernatural boldness to approach the things or people you need to address. Do not back down. Stand up and make those bold moves in life. When you do, God can use you to change not just your life but, like Moses, countless others as well. With my mind being renewed I have received the courage from God to make bold moves. Today it can happen for you.

BITE OF THE DAY

No more excuses! It is time to make bold moves in your life.

REFLECTION

What are some things that are holding you back?

Day 20
God Will Answer

"And it shall come to pass, that before they call, I will answer; and while they are yet speaking, I will hear." Isaiah 65:24

*W*hile attending primary school we had to stand in a line outside our classroom as the attendance register was marked. When our class teacher sternly called our names, we had to respond instantly by saying 'Present Sir or Miss'. If someone was absent there was a deafening silence; the student was not there therefore no answer was needed.

In 1 Kings 18:17-40 the Prophet EIijah threw the prophets of Baal a challenge to call on their god who would respond by fire. However, as the public showdown went on, the Baal prophets called, they did all they could but there was a deafening silence; Baal was not hence there was no response. On the other

57

hand, Elijah called, and God answered by fire. Our Great God is Omnipotent and present; He always answers whenever we call on Him and He stands ready to show us great and mighty things. Be encouraged today, no matter what the circumstance you may be facing God is able to answer. He has the power to show up mightily in your life.

"Call unto me, and I will answer thee, and show thee great and mighty things, which thou knowest not." Jeremiah 33:3

BITE OF THE DAY

When you call on God he will answer and show up for you.

REFLECTION

When the need arises, who do you readily call on?

Day 21
Crossover Now

"Moses my servant is dead; now therefore arise, go over this Jordan, thou, and all this people, unto the land which I do give to them, even to the children of Israel" (Joshua 1:2).

$\mathcal{A}$s I began the new believers' journey, I realized that there was a personal challenge that I had to learn. I had to cross over from where I was to where God wanted me to be. Being serious about crossing over requires maintaining discipline in investing time in the Word of God and in prayer. As they stood on the verge of entering the Promised Land, the children of Israel had to arise in their minds and leave their comfort zones.

Today God wants you to move in faith and crossover in victory. The journey of your life may seem challenging but bear in mind, you are not moving based on your own strength or sight. You are moving in bold faith and total dependence on God. When you decide to crossover you will face opposition and people will disassociate themselves from you but move out. The truth is you must continue in faith in spite of the odds. When you do, you will see God lifting you off the ground. You must arise in your mind. Do not listen to the negative comments of others. Do not allow that limited environment to rub off on you. You were created in the image of God. You have what it takes to crossover. A transformed mind opens the door to endless opportunities. It is time to crossover. It may not be easy, but it is possible. Crossover from limitations, insecurities, and a life of mediocrity. God is saying it is time to take hold of His word. Experience a life of purpose and wealth. Victory cannot be gained with an old mindset or staying in your comfort zones. The new dimensions into fulfilling your God-given purpose can only be achieved when you crossover.

BITE OF THE DAY

Take serious action to fulfil your purpose.

REFLECTION

Have you become stuck in your comfort zone?

Donna Morris
"Moved to a New Mindset: Free From Limitations,
Rejections, And Fears"

21 Days of

Transforming Affirmations

1. I take every thought captive unto the obedience of Jesus Christ, casting down every imagination, and every high and lofty thing that exalts itself against the knowledge of God. -2 Corinthians 10:5

2. I will not allow the enemy to use my mind as a garbage dump. I will not meditate on the things that he offers me. As a man thinks in his heart, so is he; therefore, all of my thoughts are positive. -Proverbs 23:7

3. I am walking by faith; I do not walk by sight. -2 Corinthians 5; 7

4. I will not speak corruptly; I will only use edifying words. -Ephesians 4:29

5. I am a doer of the Word. I will meditate on the Word all day long. -James 1:22; Psalm 1:2

6. I do not have a spirit of fear, but of power and love and a sound mind. -2 Timothy 1:7

7. I am delighting in the Word of God, and I will not forget it. -Psalms 119:16

8. My mind is at peace in Jesus Name.
   "You will keep him in perfect peace, whose mind is stayed on You, because he trusts in You.' -Isaiah 26:3

9. I am sober minded, and the loins of my mind are blessed in Jesus' Name.
   "Therefore, gird up the loins of your mind, be sober, and rest your hope fully upon the grace that is to be brought to you at the revelation of Jesus Christ;" -1 Peter 1:13

10. I set my mind on the things that are above:
    Since I have been raised together with Christ, I seek the things that are above, where Christ is, seated on the right hand of God. I set my

mind on the things that are above, not on the things that are on the earth.' -Colossians 3:1-2

11. My mind is guarded by Christ Jesus. The Peace of God rests in my heart and in my mind.

"Be anxious for nothing, but in everything by prayer and supplication, with thanksgiving, let your requests be made known to God; and the peace of God, which surpasses all understanding, will guard your hearts and minds through Christ Jesus."

-Philippians 4:6-7.

12. I have the mind of Christ:

For who has known the mind of the Lord, that he should instruct him?" But I do have Christ's mind.' -1 Corinthians 2:16.

13. I leave behind negative thinking and rise with wealthy thoughts.

14. The old mindset is gone, the new has come…
I am a new creation 2 Corinthians 5: 17

15. My strength is renewed by the eagles…
Psalms 103 :5

16. I see the Lord is doing a new thing in my life.
-Isaiah 43:19

17. I have made a new attitude adjustment in my
mind. -Ephesians 4:22-24

18. I am always on God's Mind. -Psalms 139:13

19. I am more than a conqueror… -Romans 8:37

20. I am strong and very courageous… -
Deuteronomy 31:6

21. I can do all things through Christ who strengthens me. -Philippians 4:13

Donna Morris
"Moved to a New Mindset: Free From Limitations, Rejections, And Fears"

Donna M. Morris

About the Author

*D*onna Morris is the author of "Moved to a New

Mindset " Free from Limitations, Rejections and

Fears. Ordained Minister, Certified Marriage Mentor,

The Institute of Marriage & Family Affairs (TIMFA)

Empowerment Speaker, Certified Christian Life

Coach, Founder of Scripture Drill Bible Program.

She has great passion in Prayer and Studying the

Word of God and is the founder of the Scripture Drill

Bible Programme.

She moves swiftly sharing scriptures empowering others to encounter new depths in their faith. She has a heart for young people, an avid reader, and a confidante.

Over twenty years in life insurance Industry - Guardian Life Insurance Company Jamaica

Her strongest desire is that her life will be a true reflection of Christ, thus fulfilling divine Purpose.

She is married, and a proud mother to a lovely son.

Donna M. Morris

Made in the USA
Columbia, SC
13 February 2025

53735290R00048